Mother Nature

A Bridge to Conscious Living

by Mary Jane Kasliner

© Mary Jane Kasliner 2018

All rights reserved. No part of this book may be reproduced in any form or by any means, electronic or mechanical, including photocopying, recording or any information retrieval system, without prior permission in writing from the publishers.

ISBN-10: 0-9860468-0-9

ISBN-13: 978-0-9860468-0-3

Printed in the United States of America

Formatting by

Kathrine Rend :: Rend Graphics 2018

www.rendgraphics.com

Contents

Introduction: 5

The Teacher: 8

Using the Journal: 9

Chapter 1: Trees 11

How Tree Qualities Are Reflected in Human Nature

How to Balance Tree Energy

What Can We Learn from Trees?

Meditation for Tree-Types

Contemplating Tree Energy

Applications

Tree Time

Chapter 2: Wind 33

How Wind Qualities Are Reflected in Human Nature

How to Balance Wind Energy

What Can We Learn from Wind?

Meditation for Tree-Types

Contemplating Wind Energy

Applications

Wind

Chapter 3: Sky 55

How Sky Qualities Are Reflected in Human Nature

How to Balance Sky Energy

What Can We Learn from Sky?

Meditation for Sky-Types

Contemplating Sky Energy

Applications

A New Dawn

Chapter 4: Mother Earth 77

How Earth Qualities Are Reflected in Human Nature

How to Balance Earth Energy

What Can We Learn from Mother Earth?

Meditation for Earth-Types

Contemplating Earth Energy

Applications

Sacrifice

Chapter 5: Water 99

How Water Qualities Are Reflected in Human Nature

How to Balance Water Energy

What Can We Learn from Water?

Meditation for Water-Types

Contemplating Water Energy

Applications

Flows of Laughter

Chapter 6: Fire 121

How Fire Qualities Are Reflected in Human Nature

How to Balance Fire Energy

What Can We Learn from Fire?

Meditation for Fire-Types

Contemplating Fire Energy

Applications

Fire!

Chapter 7: Mountain 143

How Mountain Qualities Are Reflected in Human Nature

How to Balance Mountain Energy

What Can We Learn from Mountain?

Meditation for Mountain-Types

Contemplating Mountain Energy

Applications

Standing

Chapter 8: Final Thoughts 165

Seeds

Appendix 168

Determine Your Force of Nature

About the Author: 170

About the Poets: 172

About the Cover Illustrator: 174

Bibliography: 175

Credits and Permissions: 176

Introduction

Some of the world's greatest sages, poets, artists, and psychologists were inspired by nature to understand the human condition. Lao Tzu, Confucius, William Wordsworth, John Keats, Percy Bysse Shelley, Leonardo Da Vinci, and Carl Jung are just a few of the greats whose nature consciousness shed light on man's spirituality.

Lao Tzu, the author of the Tao Te Ching and contemporary of Confucius during the 6th century BC, attempted to explain the Tao, which all things exist. Although difficult to put into words, its essence is a dynamic force that drives all things towards growth and evolution. Lao Tzu points out that this is best achieved by following the path of least resistance so life can unfold naturally and without interference.

In nature, nothing exists independently; rather, an interconnection occurs for the greater whole to exist. This synergistic relationship allows for the regeneration of all living things. This is like the Confucian thought process that held a basic order in the universe and a natural harmony linking man, nature, and the cosmos (heaven) together. Man, by nature, is a social being, and the order of the universe should reflect human relationships. The dominant principle of Confucian thought stressed the perfection of man as seen by the perfection in nature. The natural world reflects balance and harmony. To realize these life qualities, judgment and expectation can no longer exist as they are the root cause of suffering, bondage, and unrest.

The great poets of our time were inspired by nature. Wordsworth was deeply affected by the magnificent landscape of the natural world. For Wordsworth, nature provided a powerful influence on the human mind. The natural world, be it the tallest mountain or a blooming flower, could elicit noble thoughts. Wordsworth repeatedly emphasized the importance of nature to an individual's intellectual and spiritual development.

Leonardo Da Vinci was exemplary for utilizing his observations of nature to bring life to his paintings and drawings. Many of his inventions were inspired by observing natural phenomena. For example, Leonardo's design for a flying machine was inspired by studying the wings of birds in flight, while his designs for a parachute and helicopter were a result of his observations of seed pods and flowers falling from trees.

The famous psychologist Carl Jung connected to nature's simplistic beauty in his memoirs Memories, Dreams and Reflections. He states, "every stone, every plant, every single thing seemed alive and indescribably marvelous." It is apparent from his statement that nature is a gift. Turning to its "aliveness" heals our fragile egos and chaotic minds.

The power of nature reveals much about our human journey. The changes we see through the seasons, weather patterns, growth, and decay strengthen things, as variation is the rule of nature. Nature does not resist but rather explores its possibilities and what may become of them. Life is about change. When we embrace change, we become the instrument that plays the song of life.

When we are in sync with nature, we can overcome obstacles. The ebb and flow of ocean tides build energy. When water encounters a barrier, it finds another way. The lesson is to persevere. Serene waterways inspire peace regardless of the changes that occur on their surface.

The majestic mountains, so still and at ease, represent the virtue of strong character, while trees in bloom arouse creativity, vitality, and action. The light and warmth of fire, a gift from Prometheus, is a connection to the divine and reflects our desire to consume and destroy but is also the beacon of light that leads to a higher self.

The sky represents the dome of heaven and the zenith of creation – a productive energy for mankind. The wind, although invisible, is a gift as seen through trees swaying and birds flying. It teaches us how to be flexible and pliable in life. Finally, the earth is the feminine aspect of creation. She is the nurturer with boundless energy that connects us to our instincts, intuition, and self-sufficiency.

It is apparent nature is filled with profound knowledge. *Mother Nature – A Bridge to Conscious Living* is a seven-week journal process that captures messages from the great forces of nature through activities, applications, meditations, and inspirational poems. You will notice subtle messages from Mother Earth and Father Sky. This is a magical process. Record your thoughts in the pages of this book and use it as a guide on your life journey.

Take your time during the process as it is all about achieving a state of oneness. There are no rules. Setting restrictions will only move you further from spiritual oneness. It is inaction and non-attachment to that which lead to contentment.

Through the wisdom of God's creations are the answers to the mystery of life. Simplicity is where you will find harmony and understanding of all things. Nature has a way of piquing our curiosity and desire to know more about God. Here, we align with our true selves. In the words of Wordsworth from his famous poem Tintern Abbey:

"And I have felt a presence that disturbs me with the joy

of elevated thoughts; a sense of sublime

of something far more deeply interfused,

whose dwelling is the light of the setting suns,

And the round ocean and the living air,

And the blue sky, and in the mind of man,

A motion and spirit, that impels

All thinking things, all objects of all thought and rolls through all things."

Our connection to nature, the cosmos, and the Universe will move us toward a greater destiny. Keeping a strong connection to Mother Earth and Her bounties creates a community of life.

The Teacher

Just beyond my doorstep
Stands a sunny garden enclosed--
Property for my pleasure kept.
In cultivated rows.

Groomed in neat retention,
Arrogant, I have thought
It makes a fine possession.
It is not.

It is a waiting classroom,
An inviting gateway to all;
Made of earth and tree and bloom,
And creatures large and small.

Renae Johnson

Using the Journal

Japanese Gardens Oregon

This journal is divided into seven sections for each of the seven manifestations of nature. At the beginning of each section you will find qualities and characteristics associated with each natural manifestation along with a beautiful photograph. Next, follow the suggestions of how you can infuse the attributes of each manifestation into your life and what you can learn from it. Then, read the daily meditations and record any thoughts, changes and progress in your life as you reconnect to these powerful forces of nature. Finally, enjoy the beautiful poetry at the end of each chapter as you attune your focus inward and experience absolute stillness.

Tree arouses the sleeping seeds beneath the earth bringing all things to life.

Olympic National Park – Washington State

One

▲

Trees

*T*rees frame life. They are the largest living piece of creation on the planet with over 100,000 known species in the world covering over 9 billion acres. Their spreading roots, sturdy trunk, and flexible branches are essential to our well-being in so many ways. They fuel this planet with oxygen, keep soil from eroding, mark the seasons, have healing qualities and provide a canopy and habitat for wildlife. There dynamic beauty dapples the earth's landscape like a brush stroke across an artist canvas.

Since the beginning of time man has had a special relationship with trees. In the book of Genesis, the infamous apple tree represents the sum total of all human knowing. It encapsulates everything we learned as a species. It is the totality of everything that everyone knows and is in some shareable form.

There are countless poets and writers that speak of the power and beauty of trees. In J.R.R. Tolkien's poem *One White Tree*, he writes:

Tall ships and tall kings

Three times three.

What brought they from the foundered land

Over the flowing sea?

Seven stars and seven stones

And one white tree.

The white tree stood as a symbol of Gondor's roots and Aragon's heredity in *Lord of the Rings*. The white tree is looked upon as a powerful element that reunites the men of Gondor with Middle-earth and symbolically speaking indicates this *tree* has a long line of ancestors that ultimately leads to good winning out over evil in Middle-earth.

The famous poet, Henry Wadsworth Longfellow so poignantly writes in his poem *A Day of Sunshine*, how trees sound like a celestial symphony while the branches bend downward as the wind moves among them. Even the ancient sages found trees to be profound in their beauty and power describing them as arousing children whose roots feed from the breast of Mother Earth from where all life springs. They saw every tree as unique with some acting as a beacon of enlightenment while others were strong with endless waves of energy filled with wisdom of the ages.

We have much to learn from our *Standing Brothers and Sisters*. By reaffirming our connection to them we can embrace their wisdom and find a new sense of joy, growth and creativity in life. Trees are truly a divine gift of nature. After all, as William Cullen Bryant states; "The groves were God's first temples."

The ancient Greek philosophers theorized that every human embodies a tiny world within, and that this small, internal world (microcosm) reflects the larger world outside (macrocosm). If we use their theory of Microcosm and Macrocosm to explain the relationship between humans and nature, then we find that humans share a number of qualities with nature, as well.

How Tree Qualities Are Reflected in Human Nature

Just as a tree begins as a seed and pushes through soil, a human being begins as an egg and pushes through the birth canal—both driven by the will for growth and survival.

Trees signify vitality, concentration, initiative, quick movement, and irrepressible strength. We can identify these qualities in people who are self-starters, quick-thinkers, action-oriented, independent, imaginative, intuitive, visionary, free-spirited, and vibrant.

Those with tree energy tend to move at a frenetic pace, which can create vulnerability. In the yogic philosophy, constant movement refers to rajas (which also symbolizes passion and energy). Rajas resist the balanced nature of sattva (associated with purity and virtue), and in doing so it becomes difficult to tap into your higher self. This can create problems when it comes to finishing a job, as the finer details are left out.

A person with tree energy works best independently. If employed, they thrive in roles that allow them to channel their energy into generating new ideas. Any other position would stifle their growth. Careers that favor public speaking, carpentry, architecture, consulting, teaching, television, athletics, or inventing and innovation are a natural fit.

How to Balance Tree Energy

Though energy can be an asset, it is most productive in moderation. If you identify with tree qualities, here are a few ways to achieve greater balance:

- Take a dance class, or experiment with other ways to get your body moving.

- Collaborate with others—join a group or workshop— rather than trying to work alone always.

- Engage in yoga practice.

- Institute a daily meditation practice (Zen meditation is particularly good for tree types).

- Chant mantras to channel energy through the vocal system.

- Practice patience.

- Incorporate more vegetables and fruits into your diet, and lower the amount of oils, fats, dairy, and flour products.

What Can We Learn From Trees?

1. *To be flexible in life.* A tree's flexible branches allow it to withstand fierce weather. In flexibility there is strength and resilience. If we maintain a flexible position in our attitude and viewpoint, then we will naturally see eye-to-eye with others.

2. *Acceptance.* Trees are always changing, shedding leaves, spreading their roots and sprouting new shoots. This is what keeps them alive and filled with vitality. If you accept that change is a part of the natural order of all things, then your life will morph into a new vitality and zest for living.

3. *To take a firm stance.* The deeper a trees root system the stronger it becomes. Find what you believe in and take a firm stance. By setting your roots deep success is eminent.

4. *To be supportive.* Trees nourish and support many life forms including man. How can you support others? What qualities can you bring to the table to lead another on their soul's path?

5. *To embrace new beginnings.* The mightiest oak began as a small acorn. No matter what struggles you may have encountered in the past there is always a chance for a new beginning. Start small like the acorn and just let yourself go.

Meditation for Tree-Types

Zazen is a basic meditation, unique to Zen Buddhism, that uses the breath to focus on being present. As with any meditation practice, it is easiest to do in a quiet place, free of distractions. To begin:

- Get into a comfortable, seated position and breathe in and out of the nose.

- Notice your breath as much as possible—the quality of it, the temperature, the sensation, and the sound.

- If your mind wanders—and it will—come back to the rhythm of your breath.

- Try to remain in this meditation for at least two minutes to start. With practice, you can gradually increase the amount of time you spend in this meditation, up to 20 minutes.

Contemplating Tree Energy

The following statements are a direct result of personal meditations with tree. Take time each day to reflect upon the subtle messages you receive from these statements.

Monday:

We are the keepers of time.

Reflection: _____

_____
_____
_____
_____
_____
_____
_____
_____
_____
_____
_____
_____
_____

Contemplating Tree Energy

Reflection: _____

_____
_____
_____
_____
_____
_____
_____
_____
_____
_____
_____
_____
_____
_____
_____
_____
_____
_____
_____

Contemplating Tree Energy

Tuesday:

We are independent yet connected through our roots.

Reflection: _____

_____

_____

_____

_____

_____

_____

_____

_____

_____

_____

_____

_____

_____

Contemplating Tree Energy

Reflection: _____

_____
_____
_____
_____
_____
_____
_____
_____
_____
_____
_____
_____
_____
_____
_____
_____
_____
_____
_____
_____

Contemplating Tree Energy

Wednesday:

We uphold truth with confidence.

Reflection: _____
_____
_____
_____
_____
_____
_____
_____
_____
_____
_____
_____
_____
_____

Chapter One :: Trees

Contemplating Tree Energy

Reflection: _____

_____
_____
_____
_____
_____
_____
_____
_____
_____
_____
_____
_____
_____
_____
_____
_____
_____
_____
_____
_____
_____

Contemplating Tree Energy

Thursday:

Don't see us as only a resource. Our spirit is filled with wisdom of the ages.

Reflection: _____

_____

_____

_____

_____

_____

_____

_____

_____

_____

_____

_____

_____

_____

_____

Chapter One :: Trees

Contemplating Tree Energy

Reflection: _____

_____
_____
_____
_____
_____
_____
_____
_____
_____
_____
_____
_____
_____
_____
_____
_____
_____
_____
_____
_____
_____

Contemplating Tree Energy

Friday:

We are bound to the earth but look up to the heavens.

Reflection: _____

_____
_____
_____
_____
_____
_____
_____
_____
_____
_____
_____
_____
_____
_____
_____

Contemplating Tree Energy

Reflection: _____

_____
_____
_____
_____
_____
_____
_____
_____
_____
_____
_____
_____
_____
_____
_____
_____
_____
_____
_____

Contemplating Tree Energy

Saturday:

There is no need for ego in the tree kingdom. Even the mightiest among us is without ego.

Reflection: _____

_____
_____
_____
_____
_____
_____
_____
_____
_____
_____
_____
_____
_____

Contemplating Tree Energy

Reflection: _____

_____

_____

_____

_____

_____

_____

_____

_____

_____

_____

_____

_____

_____

_____

_____

_____

Contemplating Tree Energy

Sunday:

We are all equal no matter our size, shape, or species.

Reflection: _____

_____
_____
_____
_____
_____
_____
_____
_____
_____
_____
_____
_____
_____
_____
_____

Chapter One :: Trees

Contemplating Tree Energy

Reflection: _____

_____
_____
_____
_____
_____
_____
_____
_____
_____
_____
_____
_____
_____
_____
_____
_____
_____
_____
_____
_____
_____

Applications

Here are some suggestions for applying the wisdom of trees into your daily life.

1. Plant a tree or donate a tree to a worthy cause.

2. Decorate at least one room in your home with natural wood furnishings. Rooms that are positioned in the east, southeast or south sector of your home bode best with natural wood elements.

3. Spend time under a tree.

4. Climb a tree.

5. Build a tree house for your children or even for yourself. Go there and rest, play or simply meditate.

6. Hug a tree. Feel its bark and stroke its leaves.

7. Hang artwork or photographs with trees as a landscape.

8. Find your favorite leaf and cast a mold of it. Place the leaf mold in your home as a decoration.

TREE

Tree Time

In the cathedral of the trees

Silence is requested, Please

Whispering Woods, Buzzing Bees

Begging on my knees

Oh God -- Save these.

Ralph Ruggenbach

Mother Nature: A Bridge to Conscious Living

"And forget not that the earth delights to feel your bare feet and the winds long to play with your hair."

~Khalil Gibran

Olympic National Park – Washington State

Two

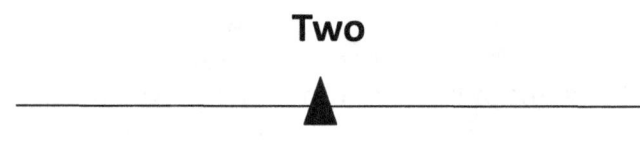

Wind

$\mathcal{A}$ir or wind together with earth, water and fire represents the substance of the world. All things rely upon wind from the light above to the waters beneath and to the smallest seed waiting to be dispersed for growth. Wind is invisible, unpredictable and life giving. It is an enigma never knowing where it begins or where it ends. As stated in the Bible: Ecclesiastes 1:6 "The wind blows to the south and turns to the north; round and round it goes, ever returning to its course."

Like the human spirit, wind has no shape or form yet its presence is known. We cannot capture the wind nor even tame it but we can feel and see its presence whether ripples on the water, leaves rustling on trees, or a butterfly fluttering its wings. For that reason, wind represents all those things that lie either beyond or beneath. It is those things we can't see in life like our soul, spirit, mind and heart.

Like the breath, wind is a source of energy that surrounds us continually connecting us to a state of being, never dying or reborn but simply being transformed. In the past wind was the energy that fueled the first explorations slowly transforming the world, and for the future it holds our destiny. This is the beauty of wind always changing so all things can be renewed. Whether it is the howling winds of a hurricane or the soothing feeling of a summer's breeze, wind moves with the ebb and flow of life challenging man to do the same; to let go of resistance and embrace life for what it is.

Wind moves in the heavens as the initiator of all things. Its upward swirling movement provides energy for life to prosper. Its essence stands for completeness, wisdom, knowledge, clarity, tranquility and contentment. It is the voice and vibrations of the earth that pushes things towards their destination, sometimes gently and other times with force. It is the conveyor of possibilities, new ideas and inspiring thoughts. Like the boughs of the willow tree or like winged creatures that soar high in the sky, wind represents graceful flow. When we choose to move gracefully through life even when the unexpected arises, growth is the result. In the words of William Arthur Ward: "The pessimist complains about the wind, the optimist expects it to change; the realist adjusts the sails." I believe the element of wind wants us to simply adjust our sails and ride the waves.

How Wind Qualities Are Reflected in Human Nature

Wind can come as a gentle breeze or a violent storm. Its unpredictability is associated with uncertainty and struggling to make one's mark. Its capriciousness, however, comes with a sense of wonderment, innocence, and clarity.

In nature, the wind disseminates seeds and plays a vital role in helping plants reproduce. This is not unlike people who gather information and effectively communicate it to others.

Wind can also be overwhelming—it can send things into disarray, or even take your breath away. Those who resonate with wind energy may find that they have a constant stream of new ideas but become paralyzed easily when the time comes to act on them; this creates stress, procrastination, and hesitation. But just as the wind picks back up, new ideas keep flowing, and with them, new opportunities to act. When ideas come, it is best for wind-types to apply their knack for scientific and philosophical thinking. This will help them focus and follow through.

Albeit wind appears to act independently, it relies on the support of the atmosphere. Those who identify with wind energy may strive for independence, but they need the support of others to achieve success. This is especially the case for those who doubt their strength. By abdicating control to someone who is more knowledgeable, they can act with greater confidence. This type of thinking lends itself to careers in consulting or advertising.

Wind's unpredictable nature also gravitates toward unstable relationships, and they may find this area of life to be a challenge. Willing to wait only so long for a relationship to work out, wind-types would rather move on until the right person shows up.

How to Balance Wind Energy

Wind requires stability to maintain a state of equilibrium. Here are some ways to achieve balance:

- Consult your common sense.
- Set deadlines to complete tasks.
- Keep your environment neat and organized.
- Engage in active exercise, such as jogging, walking, or swimming.
- Infuse dark leafy greens, seaweed, and calcium-rich foods into your diet.
- Try slow-moving forms of exercise, such as yoga, tai chi, and qigong.

What Can We Learn From Wind?

1. *How to let go and be free.* Wind does not resist but rather is free in spirit. When we let go of resistance life is joyful and we are blessed abundantly.

2. *To rely on our intuition.* This is the voice of the higher self, the sage, the seer, and the impeccable word. When we listen to higher self and use "the word" impeccably, then we experience heaven on earth.

3. *To become the dreamer, the creator and initiator in life.* This is the freedom within that stirs our natural talents and souls path. When we dream and follow that dream then we find it simple to be the initiator and creator in life.

4. *To lose routine and go with the flow.* Wind is changeable. No two days are the same for the spirit of the wind. When we stick to a daily routine we stop growing, become stagnant, and lose interest in life. So let go of routine and try something new for a change.

5. *To be subtle and a rebel.* Wind spirit is unpredictable – strong as a storm one day yet meek as a mouse the next. Wind knows itself and is comfortable with self. We too should become unpredictable. Know what we stand for even if it means to be a rebel, then so be it.

Meditation for Wind-Types

Wind is like the breath—it fuels life. Use this simple meditation to harness your power through breath work:

- Focus your attention on your lungs, as if only your lungs exist.

- Take a deep breath and note how the air is sweet, pleasant, and filled with love.

- Savor the feeling as your lungs expand.

- Fill your lungs fully, until your body surrenders through exhalation.

- Notice how relaxed and fulfilled you feel with each complete inhalation and exhalation.

- Continue this deep breathing for several minutes. Try to focus on feelings of love as you take each breath through your day.

Contemplating Wind Energy

The following statements are a result of personal meditations with wind. Take time each day to reflect upon the subtle messages you receive from these meditations.

Monday:

I am free an unabashed mysteriously moving through the Universe.

Reflection: _____

_____
_____
_____
_____
_____
_____
_____
_____
_____
_____
_____
_____
_____

Chapter Two :: Wind

Contemplating Wind Energy

Reflection: _____

_____
_____
_____
_____
_____
_____
_____
_____
_____
_____
_____
_____
_____
_____
_____
_____
_____
_____
_____
_____
_____
_____
_____

Contemplating Wind Energy

Tuesday:

I can be still as a winter's night or violent as a lion's roar.

Reflection: _____

_____

_____

_____

_____

_____

_____

_____

_____

_____

_____

_____

_____

_____

_____

_____

Contemplating Wind Energy

Reflection: _____

_____
_____
_____
_____
_____
_____
_____
_____
_____
_____
_____
_____
_____
_____
_____
_____
_____
_____
_____
_____
_____
_____
_____

Contemplating Wind Energy

Wednesday:

I am judged daily by man in so many ways. Why can't you just accept my changeability? Is that not what man must do to find peace with self?

Reflection: _____

_____
_____
_____
_____
_____
_____
_____
_____
_____
_____
_____
_____
_____

Contemplating Wind Energy

Reflection: _____

Contemplating Wind Energy

Thursday:

There is grace in my existence.

Reflection: _____

Chapter Two :: Wind

Contemplating Wind Energy

Reflection: _____

_____
_____
_____
_____
_____
_____
_____
_____
_____
_____
_____
_____
_____
_____
_____
_____
_____
_____
_____

Contemplating Wind Energy

Friday:

I have a whimsical nature and carefree existence.

Reflection: _____

_____
_____
_____
_____
_____
_____
_____
_____
_____
_____
_____
_____
_____
_____
_____
_____

Chapter Two :: Wind

Contemplating Wind Energy

Reflection: _____

_____
_____
_____
_____
_____
_____
_____
_____
_____
_____
_____
_____
_____
_____
_____
_____
_____
_____
_____
_____
_____

Contemplating Wind Energy

Saturday:

I am the breath of life with no beginning and no end.

Reflection: _____

_____
_____
_____
_____
_____
_____
_____
_____
_____
_____
_____
_____
_____
_____
_____

Contemplating Wind Energy

Reflection: _____

Contemplating Wind Energy

Sunday:

I am an enigma to many and a beacon of light to others.

Reflection: _____
_____
_____
_____
_____
_____
_____
_____
_____
_____
_____
_____
_____
_____

Contemplating Wind Energy

Reflection: _____
_____
_____
_____
_____
_____
_____
_____
_____
_____
_____
_____
_____
_____
_____
_____
_____
_____
_____

Applications

Here are some suggestions on how you can experience wind energy in your daily life.

1. Breathe in and then breathe out. Notice the rhythm of the breath in every moment.
2. Fly a kite. Notice the visual appeal the kite takes from the wind dynamics.
3. Tilt your head back while swinging on a swing.
4. Take a ride with the windows down.
5. Enjoy a walk along the beach.
6. Ride a bicycle.
7. Hang a wind chime in a tree.
8. Run down a hill.
9. Sit under a tree and enjoy the swaying branches.
10. Go sailing and enjoy the sensation of wind on your mind and body.
11. Take a hot air balloon ride.
12. Go hang gliding or parasailing.

WIND

Wind

Between us, Home is

The wind, the cars, the kids,

and the street.

Hearten your window;

Line it with books,

plants and pens.

Pull down that thick

shade, so the sun can't

come in. And listen:

Over the kids, the cars, and the

street—there is always

the wind.

Christina Garofalo

"When you realize how perfect things are you will tilt your head back and laugh at the sky."

~Buddha

Victoria, Canada

Three

▲

Sky

*Wh*at is sky? This is a question that lends itself to much discussion. As children we looked up to the sky while lying on the ground wondering who was up in this vast place and how did one get there. In our minds it was a place where God lived; a place where Jack climbed up the giant bean stalk and arrived in a land so high; a place where angels flew and clouds floated for days on end.

Sky is a place where we can spread our imaginary wings and literally reach for the stars. It is a place where possibilities are born and divine guidance is available. So the question still remains "What is sky?" Scientifically we know sky is part of the atmosphere or outer space. We know it takes on a pale blue color because air scatters sunlight molecules. But for man the sky is an intriguing place. So many stars and planets to observe in the hopes of finding other life form, a quest if you will to find God. It is an omnipotence part of the world that constantly awakens man's desire to seek knowledge and to understand the universe.

Many cultures throughout the world including Greek mythology honor sky for all its bounty and blessings. Zeus, lord of the sky, ruled the wind, rain, thunder and lightning to keep peace in the heavens for centuries. Shamans of South America honor *father sky* through ritual ceremonies offering food, wine and incense to invoke its spirit. Even when a new bottle of liquor is opened, the top portion is placed in a separate container and taken outside and offered to Father Heaven and Mother Earth.

In Hinduism sky is the fifth element and considered to be the stuff celestial beings are made up of. It is considered to be an indestructible component of man's soul and the purest element of all. It acts as a medium for man to communicate with the gods using sound vibrations through the chanting of mantras. It is from the sky the gods displayed their awesome powers through weather patterns. Sky is that place where man ascends at death to join the gods and their ancestors.

The bedrock of eastern cultures is based on polar opposites or halves. The sky and earth are complimentary parts that interact for harmony to exist. One half not being superior to the other but rather they co-exist depending upon one another for balance to ensue. All things move towards these polar points and can be aligned to each pole. Human spirit is part of heaven or sky, whereas physical body is part of mother earth. Everything in the universe as we know it has a naturally occurring counterpart to maintain equilibrium. Sky then maintains the equilibrium of the earth as she receives its boundless energy.

The enigma of the sky element continues to intrigue man to search for the ultimate truth. It is likened to the vastness of the human mind. When man is fully capable to tap into the spirit of his mind he will come to know the workings of the universe where sky resides. Sky is a boundless being that upholds all.

How Sky Qualities Are Reflected in Human Nature

People with sky energy are natural leaders and take on a father-like role in life. However, maintaining high levels of responsibility and competence, over time, can lead to self-criticism or self-sabotage.

People with sky energy can lead at the highest level; you'll often find them at the head of large corporations or nations. Their lofty ideals, rational thinking, good judgment, and organized minds make them apt to tackle any challenge. It is important, however, that those who favor sky energy resist their egotistical nature and focus their intentions and ideas on the greater good. Otherwise, the high expectations they place on others can strain their personal relationships.

By and large, sky behavior in human beings comes with a strong sense of morality and a need to connect to their community. Spirituality and intuition are their greatest assets when working with society. Order is essential for sky-types.

How to Balance Sky Energy

Sky energy is associated with strong physical health, but the pressures of leadership can cause high levels of stress, which eventually takes its toll. Sky people do best with the following:

- Relaxation techniques to calm the mind.

- Yoga poses that invert the body to move blood flow up towards the head.

- A diet rich in fennel, peppers, okra, broccoli, carrots, cauliflower, free–range chicken, and turnips.

- Group meditation classes.

What Can We Learn From Sky?

1. *Leadership skills.* Father sky is a natural leader inspiring man to search, explore and seek knowledge. Father sky implores us to "reach for the stars" and become the inspiration for those to follow. Good leaders are not born but rather develop through a never ending process of self-study, education, training and experience. This is what Father sky teaches man; its' all about how to "inspire" or be "in spirit."

2. *To be colorful.* Father sky is a chameleon changing its backdrop from blue, to pink, purple, orange, yellow and black. Father sky doesn't conform but rather reaches out capturing the spirit of nature. Man can learn from father sky by letting his personality become boundless, full of life, well rounded, interesting and happy go lucky.

3. *To be free spirited.* Father sky is limitless and content with self. To let go completely means to let go of what others may think, to release conventional behavior, not to let anything bog you down. Father sky implores us to march to the beat of our own drum.

4. *To be in awe of life.* Father sky has always been a source of wonder for man with its seemingly limitless amount of energy and power. If we change our perspective in life and begin to look at all things with "awe" and "wonder" we will find that everything in life is amazing, filled with surprise, and joyful.

5. *To seek quietude.* Whether a dark starry night, cloudy day or sun drenched sky; heaven's dome is a source of quietude. The stillness within the movement exudes a sense of tranquility and grace that transcends all things. By practicing daily meditation man can achieve stillness within the movement of life. It is in this stillness where contentment is found.

Meditation for Sky-Types

Sky represents the heavenly father and creator. It requires the energy of the earth for balance and to manifest our desires. Nodi Shodhana pranayama (or alternate breath) is an effective way to bring about calm and balance:

- Sit comfortably with your spine erect and shoulders relaxed.
- Place your left hand on your left knee, palms open to the sky or in chin mudra (thumb and index finger gently touching at the tips) to create a receptive state in which you can connect to your higher self.
- Place the tip of the index finger and middle finger of the right hand in between the eyebrows, the ring finger and little finger on the left nostril, and the thumb on the right nostril. You can use the ring finger and little finger to open or close the left nostril and the thumb for the right nostril. (For simplification, you can just use your thumb and ring finger to close off the nostrils).
- Press your thumb down on the right nostril and breathe out gently through the left nostril.
- Now breathe in from the left nostril and press the left nostril gently with the ring finger and little finger. Removing the right thumb from the right nostril, breathe out from the right.
- Breathe in from the right nostril and exhale through the left. You have now completed round one. Continue inhaling and exhaling from alternate nostrils.
- Complete nine rounds like this (or as many as you like), by alternately breathing through both nostrils. After every exhalation, remember to breathe in through the same nostril from which you just exhaled. Keep your eyes closed throughout and continue taking long, smooth breaths. Don't force it.
- When you are finished, return to your natural breath.

Contemplating Sky Energy

The following statements are a result of personal meditations with sky. Take time each day to reflect upon the subtle messages you receive from these meditations.

Monday:

I am filled with abundance, knowledge and possibilities.

Reflection: _____

_____

_____

_____

_____

_____

_____

_____

_____

_____

_____

_____

_____

Contemplating Sky Energy

Reflection: _____

_____
_____
_____
_____
_____
_____
_____
_____
_____
_____
_____
_____
_____
_____
_____
_____
_____
_____
_____
_____
_____
_____

Contemplating Sky Energy

Tuesday:

I am the wonder seen on a child's face.

Reflection: _____

_____
_____
_____
_____
_____
_____
_____
_____
_____
_____
_____
_____
_____
_____

Contemplating Sky Energy

Reflection: _____

_____
_____
_____
_____
_____
_____
_____
_____
_____
_____
_____
_____
_____
_____
_____
_____
_____
_____
_____
_____
_____
_____
_____

Contemplating Sky Energy

Wednesday:

It is through my presence that you will find your natural state of being.

Reflection: _____

Contemplating Sky Energy

Reflection: _____

Contemplating Sky Energy

Thursday:

I am the dome of heaven that covers the earth. It is here where the luminaries shine for all to see. The sun, moon and stars dapple my surface like jewels upon a princess's crown.

Reflection: _____

_____

_____

_____

_____

_____

_____

_____

_____

_____

_____

_____

_____

_____

Contemplating Sky Energy

Reflection: _____

_____
_____
_____
_____
_____
_____
_____
_____
_____
_____
_____
_____
_____
_____
_____
_____
_____
_____
_____
_____
_____
_____
_____

Contemplating Sky Energy

Friday:

I am all encompassing and awe inspiring.

Reflection: _____
_____
_____
_____
_____
_____
_____
_____
_____
_____
_____
_____
_____
_____
_____
_____

Contemplating Sky Energy

Reflection: _____

_____
_____
_____
_____
_____
_____
_____
_____
_____
_____
_____
_____
_____
_____
_____
_____
_____
_____
_____
_____
_____
_____
_____

Contemplating Sky Energy

Saturday:

I am spirit that lies within.

Reflection: _____

Contemplating Sky Energy

Reflection: _____

_____
_____
_____
_____
_____
_____
_____
_____
_____
_____
_____
_____
_____
_____
_____
_____
_____
_____
_____
_____
_____
_____
_____
_____

Contemplating Sky Energy

Sunday:

I am the seed of all creation.

Reflection: _____

_____

_____

_____

_____

_____

_____

_____

_____

_____

_____

_____

_____

_____

_____

Chapter Three :: Sky

Contemplating Sky Energy

Reflection: _____
_____
_____
_____
_____
_____
_____
_____
_____
_____
_____
_____
_____
_____
_____
_____
_____
_____
_____
_____

Applications

Here are some suggestions of how you can bring sky energy into your life.

1. Look through a telescope and stargaze.
2. Take a Ferris wheel ride.
3. Grab a window seat on your next flight.
4. Take a hot air balloon ride.
5. Look up to the sky, watch the clouds pass, and notice how it calms the mind.
6. Go bird watching.
7. Watch the sunrise and set.
8. Observe a thunder storm.
9. Watch a plane fly.
10. Go parachute jumping.

SKY

A New Dawn

Indigo velvet

hushed and still

fading to violet

at day's spill

sneaking silent

ending night's fill

Dawn's onset

giving thrill.

Ralph Roggenbuck

"The mountains, rivers, earth, grasses, trees and forests are always emanating a subtle, precious light, day and night, always emanating a subtle, precious sound, demonstrating and expounding to all people the unsurpassed ultimate truth."

~Unknown

Columbia River Gorge – Oregon

Four

Mother Earth

*E*arth is the third planet from the sun, approximately 4.5 billion years old, and the only planet that harbors life. As the jewel of the solar system, it is home to over 6.5 billion people and trillions of other life form.

Gaia known as Mother Earth was the first Greek God who was actually a Goddess. It was said She created herself out of primordial chaos where all life sprang and where all shall return after a life span ends. She is a living system with consciousness whose entire ecosystem is personified through nature. The Gaia principle developed by Dr. Lovelock in the 60's demonstrates this concept. According to Dr. Lovelock, man is a part of nature and nature is a part of man; therefore God is part of man and everywhere, and everything is God. The Gaia principle sees the planet earth as alive with a soul and not just a hunk of rock orbiting around the sun. This is not an uncommon belief, as many indigenous people around the world honor this viewpoint including the late St. Francis of Assisi. St. Francis preached how the whole world is a family connected through Mother Earth as care giver, sister moon, brother fire, and father God above who provide the elements of nature that lead us all back to Him. God is revealed through the beauty and diversity found in nature. He is the mirror of nature and by loving all aspects of nature leads us to divine source.

The Native American Indians also honor every part of the earth. Everything is sacred about the earth. In 1854 the *Great White Chief* from Washington so eloquently stated:

> " *Every part of the earth is sacred to my people.*
> *Every shining pine needle, every sandy shore, every mist in the dark woods, every clearing and humming insect is holy in the memory and experience of my people. We are part of the earth and it is part of us. The perfumed flowers are our sisters: the deer, the horse, the great eagle, these are our brothers. The rocky crests, the juiced in the meadows, the body heat of the pony, and man - all belong to the same family."*

What a beautiful testament to nature letting man know he is not above nature but sits on the same side with Her.

The Q'ero people from Peru share a similar belief honoring Pachamama, meaning Mother Earth, for her bounties. They believe nature was given to man from father sky and is the teacher on how to live one's life. The basic premise is to freely give back to Mother with gratitude and in return abundance is received.

The Q'ero's belief is in alignment with the energetic laws of the universe which captures the concept of conscious living. They believe Pachamama speaks to us through her symbols, sights and sounds and is the key to understanding the Universe. Even though man has developed much technology, it is clear how the natural environment still manages to capture a sense of awe and amazement for us. Nature still holds great mysteries that man may never be able to unravel. But by regaining our close connection to nature man can begin to disseminate these mysteries.

Today, there is an emerging movement to explore mankind's desire to reconnect to the earth. This is being done through natural architecture. To design with nature in mind draws man closer to the earth. Of course this is not a new concept. The famous American architect, Frank Lloyd Wright, designed thousands of structures which were in harmony with humanity and its environment. Fortunately, many architects today are upholding this design approach as a way to capture the harmonious link between man and nature. These organic building designs take on the simplistic beauty of Mother Nature leaving behind high technology connecting man's vibrations to that of nature's.

Mother Earth teaches us to persevere even when things seem impossible. If we are open to a solution then one will be presented as the earth follows heaven's time and heaven's time helps the earth. If we yield to the earth and treat Her with kindness unlimited abundance is ours. If we choose to insult Her, then we choose to insult ourselves. Without precious earth, heaven's creativity dissipates without being realized. In the words of Martin Luther:

> *"God writes the gospel not in the Bible alone,*
> *but on trees and flowers and clouds and stars."*

How Earth Qualities Are Reflected in Human Nature

Mother Earth is the primal nurturer. She is receptive, strong, and gentle. Together, earth and sky complement one another, and in doing so, foster creation.

People who connect closely to their environment, strive to maintain order, and are conservative in their actions will resonate naturally with earth energy. These people also tend to be grounded, centered, supportive, warm, humble, and in touch with their emotions. Their attention to detail, especially when it comes to basic needs—food, clothing, shelter, and other domestic concerns—are first and foremost on their agenda.

The earth-type is committed to pleasing and accommodating the needs of others. Their innate patience and honesty attracts others to them, including strays. This doesn't matter to the earth person; their "for-service" outlook gives others a basis from which to grow.

A person with earth energy works best when they combine their efforts with others rather than taking the lead. They tend to a group or organization with dedication and zeal to prove they can achieve the end goal. However, just as Mother Earth requires the respect of humankind, earth-types look for acknowledgment and respect; without it, they pull away and lose confidence.

Earth-types are compassionate and serve all life forms unconditionally. Because they are frequently tempted to serve others for their own gratification, it's important for them to check in with the needs of others, to ensure that it is not just themselves who receive the benefits. This will clear obstacles and inspire spiritual growth.

Careers that serve others, including teaching, therapy, nursing, medicine, assisting, environmental work, and farming, are a natural fit.

How to Balance Earth Energy

Earth energy is wonderful when it comes to caring for others, but it's not great when it comes to caring for yourself. Earth-types find it difficult to tune into their own needs, because they place a disproportionate amount of energy on the problems of others. If you identify with earth energy, incorporate the following for self-care:

- A diet that includes brussels sprouts, celery root, radicchio, artichokes, beets, chicory, endive, sweet potatoes, asparagus, kohlrabi, avocado, beans, lean beef, turkey, and veal.

- Daily exercise that focuses on circulation and moving bodily fluids, such as step aerobics to move lymphatic fluid.

- A meditation practice that includes prayer and mindfulness.

- Lymphatic massage.

What Can We Learn From Mother Earth?

1. *Love and respect.* Mother Earth has respect for all who live upon her. There is no part of her that is greater than another. All is one and perfect. We are kin to all living things and therefore must love and show respect to one another. We must regard one another with esteem and consideration.

2. *Gain wisdom.* The greatest sages known to man walked upon the earth. In their very footsteps lies the wisdom to be shared with all. When we take time with mother earth we too shall learn the ways of the sages and find the wisdom that upholds ones spirit.

3. *Develop courage.* Mother earth does not falter when shaken. Every day *She* provides for all without compromise. We too must work through the difficult times and defend what is right, what we believe in, and be a part of this world.

4. *Be honest.* The earth is pure in nature, true to the core. We too should be honest in our actions and project good feelings from the heart letting go of deceitful behavior.

5. *Practice humility.* The earth does not rank different aspects as being better than another. All parts are equal. Man must realize that no one is superior to another rather we are all equal. We should honor our differences, our talents, and share in our accomplishments.

6. *Seek truth.* The earth is always true to itself. It does not seek to destroy. This is a quality that man needs to fully grasp. If we are true to self first then it will be easy to be true to others.

7. *Unconditional love.* Mother earth loves unconditionally. There is nothing she will not give to all who seek her. So too must man love his fellow brother and sister without conditions and share with all.

Meditation for Earth-Types

Earth represents the mother, nurturer, and liberating current; it requires sky energy (the father) for balance and to bring intentions to fruition. The following meditation aims to recharge the earth person, so they can better serve themselves and others:

- Sit comfortably with your spine erect and shoulders relaxed.
- Soften the corners of your eyes.
- Focus on the ebb and flow of the breath.
- Repeat the simple mantra, "I am divine love" 108 times to affirm connection to love and align ourselves to the will of the universe. This calms the mind, body, and soul.

Contemplating Earth Energy

The following statements are a result of personal meditations with Mother Earth. Take time each day to reflect upon the subtle messages you receive from these meditations.

Monday:

I seek to nourish your desires and heal you from the inside out.

Reflection: _____

_____
_____
_____
_____
_____
_____
_____
_____
_____
_____
_____
_____

Chapter Four :: Mother Earth

Contemplating Earth Energy

Reflection: _____

_____
_____
_____
_____
_____
_____
_____
_____
_____
_____
_____
_____
_____
_____
_____
_____
_____
_____
_____
_____
_____

Contemplating Earth Energy

Tuesday:

I am more than the soil that covers my body. I am a living being with consciousness that holds the key to evolution.

Reflection: _____

_____

_____

_____

_____

_____

_____

_____

_____

_____

_____

_____

_____

_____

Contemplating Earth Energy

Reflection: _____

_____
_____
_____
_____
_____
_____
_____
_____
_____
_____
_____
_____
_____
_____
_____
_____
_____
_____
_____
_____
_____
_____
_____

Contemplating Earth Energy

Wednesday:

You can come to me to rest your weariness and release your suffering.

Reflection: _____
_____
_____
_____
_____
_____
_____
_____
_____
_____
_____
_____
_____
_____
_____
_____

Chapter Four :: Mother Earth

Contemplating Earth Energy

Reflection: _____

_____
_____
_____
_____
_____
_____
_____
_____
_____
_____
_____
_____
_____
_____
_____
_____
_____
_____
_____
_____
_____
_____

Contemplating Earth Energy

Thursday:

I am everywhere. I am the Mandala of life, the yin and the yang continually transforming the seeds of life.

Reflection: _____

Contemplating Earth Energy

Reflection: _____

_____
_____
_____
_____
_____
_____
_____
_____
_____
_____
_____
_____
_____
_____
_____
_____
_____
_____
_____
_____
_____
_____

Contemplating Earth Energy

Friday:

When you connect to me you will find oneness and peace in your heart. It is through nature that the divine spirit lives and breathes.

Reflection: _____

_____

_____

_____

_____

_____

_____

_____

_____

_____

_____

_____

Chapter Four :: Mother Earth

Contemplating Earth Energy

Reflection: _____

_____
_____
_____
_____
_____
_____
_____
_____
_____
_____
_____
_____
_____
_____
_____
_____
_____
_____
_____
_____
_____
_____

Contemplating Earth Energy

Saturday:

Bring me into your life. Spend time with me. Speak to me and I will listen. Respect me as I do you and you shall find peace with self and others.

Reflection: _____

_____

_____

_____

_____

_____

_____

_____

_____

_____

_____

_____

_____

_____

Chapter Four :: Mother Earth

Contemplating Earth Energy

Reflection: _____

_____
_____
_____
_____
_____
_____
_____
_____
_____
_____
_____
_____
_____
_____
_____
_____
_____
_____
_____

Contemplating Earth Energy

Sunday:

Seek me daily for right mind and spirit. I am your father's creation subtle like the breath.

Reflection: _____

_____
_____
_____
_____
_____
_____
_____
_____
_____
_____
_____
_____
_____

Contemplating Earth Energy

Reflection: _____

_____
_____
_____
_____
_____
_____
_____
_____
_____
_____
_____
_____
_____
_____
_____
_____
_____
_____
_____
_____
_____
_____
_____
_____

Applications

Here are some suggestions of how to explore Mother Earth.

1. Walk barefoot on mother earth.
2. Lie on a grassy field.
3. Place your ear close to the earth and LISTEN.
4. Take up yoga or qi gong practices.
5. Take a hike through the woods.
6. Spend time every day outdoors.
7. Start a rock collection.
8. Walk along the beach.
9. Plant a garden.
10. Go camping.

EARTH

Sacrifice

In the earth beneath my feet,

Sacrifice is complete.
With elements in tune,

The cycles resume,
As life gives way to life.

Dying, then alive and new—

I see this as my path, too.

A binding past can be set free,

To feed a future that is yet to be,

As life gives way to life.

Renae Johnson

"*Water is the driving force of all nature.*"
~Leonardo da Vinci

Latourell Falls – Oregon

Five

Water

Since the beginning of time water has had a central place in the practice of religion. Shamans, Priests and Seers used water for healing and cleansing the soul of impurities. In the Coqui scripture, a religion and way of life for the Coqui people, water is honored and loved. It is a living conscious entity that thinks and feels and responds to loving kind thoughts.

Dr. Emoto, a practicing physician of alternative medicine in Tokyo, has performed countless studies on the energy of water. His findings have shown that water has an intrinsic vibration pattern that emits an aura that is easily impacted by all surrounding objects including man. On a basic level, when a positive aura interacts with the water's aura, then healthy water with healing properties is the result. Can it be that water is trying to send us a message? One thing is for sure, we know human life is directly connected to the quality of water within and around us.

If Dr. Emoto's theory is correct then this could explain the healing qualities at the famous springs in Lourdes, France. Prayerful intention and the positive vibration from these prayers is what makes those springs so powerful, as the mineral content is insignificant when it comes to comparing it to other springs.

If we maintain the theory that water is a living conscious entity then it behooves man to show respect and gratitude for the life sustaining qualities it provides and the power it has to tunnel through mountains, carve landscapes, and form large ecosystems. In all its glory, water flows across this planet in the oceans, seas, lakes, rivers, ponds and streams feeding and fueling all things in its path. It is through its wisdom that has been encapsulated in mother earth since the dawn of time that man stands to learn much. Every time we encounter this basic element be it through swimming, washing or simply listening to the sounds of a plunging waterfall, gentle trickling stream, graceful lapping riverbed, or the pitter patter of rain fall, we have opportunity to gain insight about its divine essence and our own.

Water is also a source of creativity and love. It passes heaven's possibilities on for man to draw upon without exhausting the source. Its' pure and transformational qualities assist in the renewal process for man through reflection and intuition. Heaven uses the water element to tell us things and in turn water resonates to our vibrations and emotions and stores them long afterwards. When we move with the gravity and rhythm of water we experience the depth of our soul; a place that is ever changing and flowing.

How Water Qualities Are Reflected in Human Nature

Water represents the primal state, before growth. In human behavior, water is the deep thinker—one who is introspective, measured, adaptable, free, resourceful, experienced, and mature. The water person prefers solitude, but not exclusion. Through their eyes, life is varied, challenging, and changeable; they thrive on life's ebb and flow. When they resist change, they experience paralyzing fear that prevents them from moving forward.

When it comes to relationships, water-types tend to hold on tightly and can become possessive to the point of compromising their own identity. Effective communication—a trait that comes easily to people with water energy—can provide the support needed to balance those tendencies. Water-types are also very sensual and sexually active. They like to heighten their own pleasures and enjoy bringing pleasure to their partner.

Water people work better independently rather than in a group setting. This doesn't mean they can't be part of an organization—they are known to keep projects flowing in the right direction, and they are brilliant at evaluating processes and setting standards. They are more productive, however, without someone looking over their shoulder. This allows them to take risks.

Because communication comes naturally to water-types, they do well in jobs that require those skills. They are also well-equipped to handle money, and in their personal lives they spend wisely, often on enjoyable things. This makes them efficient financial planners, bankers, managers, and entrepreneurs.

Those who identify with water are drawn to change, so life can feel fast-paced. This can present a spiritual challenge, as they get caught up in mindless chatter that prevents them from identifying necessary lessons. It behooves the water person to relax and tune into their higher selves.

How to Balance Water Energy

The introspective and changeable nature of water can make it challenging to learn to let go. Their greatest lesson is to learn to be in the moment. Some ways to achieve this include:

- Breathing techniques to relax the mind.

- Guided meditations.

- Activities, such as swimming and yoga, that keep the joints and ligaments fluid.

- Practice prioritizing and following through on commitments.

- A diet rich in fiber and foods like garlic, leeks, celery root, radish, green onions, turnips, free–range chicken, cabbage, sea vegetables, seafood, and pork.

What Can We Learn From Water?

1. *Fluidity.* Water takes the path of least resistance. It simply follows the path laid out before it making no judgments, just quietly finding its destination. In order to have less stress and more joy in life, then man must let go of resistance and the need to constantly judge.

2. *Tenacity.* Water never gives up when it comes to doing its job. Tributaries feed the rivers, and the rivers feed the lakes and streams. So too should man persevere and look for assistance along the path.

3. *Humility.* Water is one of the most powerful elements; it is life sustaining and comprises 70% of the earth's surface area yet it is modest when it comes to its importance. Water is giving of itself and expects nothing in return. This is what humility is all about. By letting go of self importance one is able to see the path to helping others while fulfilling one's desires.

4. *Abundance.* There is an abundance of water in this home we call planet earth. And in these waters there is an abundance of life that sustains life forms including man. Trusting in this abundance reminds man that the universe will always provide. Trusting in the ever flowing waters of life will bring a life of abundance.

5. *Healing.* Water has a natural healing quality with its soothing, pure, weightless touch. Its intention to heal, nurture and cleanse moves deep into spirit. Man has the ability to be even a greater healer by allowing his spirit to engage with fellow man's spirit. The way of pure energy can and will heal all that is in "dis-ease."

Meditation for Water-Types

Water represents entering the unknown. This can arouse fear and is therefore best treated with introspection and a grounding meditation, like the following:

- Sit comfortably with your spine erect and shoulders relaxed.

- Become aware of your body and what and how you feel.

- Tune into the sounds around you, how the ground feels beneath you, and the quality of your breath.

- Let the mind descend into the body, as though it is positioned at the base of your spine.

- Become grounded: Imagine your pelvic bone has deep roots that penetrate the earth beneath you.

- Remain in this position for at least 10 minutes before opening your eyes and looking down at the earth.

Contemplating Water Energy

The following statements are a result of personal meditations with water. Take time each day to reflect upon the subtle messages you receive from these meditations.

Monday:

I can be shallow or deep, calm or rough, but most of all I am a resource for man and animal alike.

Reflection: _____

_____
_____
_____
_____
_____
_____
_____
_____
_____
_____
_____
_____

Contemplating Water Energy

Reflection: _____

_____
_____
_____
_____
_____
_____
_____
_____
_____
_____
_____
_____
_____
_____
_____
_____
_____
_____
_____
_____
_____

Contemplating Water Energy

Tuesday:

I am like a chameleon – always changing my appearance.

Reflection: _____

Contemplating Water Energy

Reflection: _____

_____
_____
_____
_____
_____
_____
_____
_____
_____
_____
_____
_____
_____
_____
_____
_____
_____
_____
_____
_____
_____
_____
_____

Contemplating Water Energy

Wednesday:

I am the elixir of life.

Reflection: _____
_____
_____
_____
_____
_____
_____
_____
_____
_____
_____
_____
_____
_____
_____
_____

Contemplating Water Energy

Reflection: _____

_____
_____
_____
_____
_____
_____
_____
_____
_____
_____
_____
_____
_____
_____
_____
_____
_____
_____
_____
_____
_____
_____
_____
_____

Contemplating Water Energy

Thursday:

I erode what is overwhelming and feed the depleted.

Reflection: _____
_____
_____
_____
_____
_____
_____
_____
_____
_____
_____
_____
_____
_____
_____
_____

Chapter Five :: Water

Contemplating Water Energy

Reflection: _____

_____
_____
_____
_____
_____
_____
_____
_____
_____
_____
_____
_____
_____
_____
_____
_____
_____
_____
_____
_____
_____
_____
_____

Contemplating Water Energy

Friday:

I ebb and flow like the tides of life.

Reflection: _____

Chapter Five :: Water

Contemplating Water Energy

Reflection: _____

_____
_____
_____
_____
_____
_____
_____
_____
_____
_____
_____
_____
_____
_____
_____
_____
_____
_____
_____
_____
_____
_____
_____

Contemplating Water Energy

Saturday:

I cleanse the body and spirit and make all things new.

Reflection: _____
_____
_____
_____
_____
_____
_____
_____
_____
_____
_____
_____
_____
_____
_____

WATER

Flows of Laughter

live,

laugh,

love,

in the water.

live

life,

in the ocean.

love

laughing,

in the river.

laugh

a life

time in

the pool

sprinkle

love

in the

pond

live, laugh and love for life,

we are water,

soon we will evaporate,

and

be gone.

Calvin Chance

"Labor to keep alive in your breast that little spark of celestial fire, called conscience."

~George Washington

Puget Sound Seattle, Washington

Six

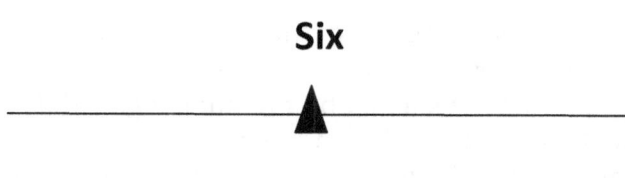

Fire

*I*n ancient Greek mythology, there is a myth that Prometheus created man by mixing earth and water together and Athena breathed air into this mixture imbuing it with spirit and soul. Prometheus added the higher soul with the element of fire that he borrowed from the wheel of the sun. It is said that the fire in our soul is akin to celestial fire (as above, so below), bringing a divine warmth to the human soul. Heraclitus, the ancient Greek philosopher also believed the human soul was comprised of fire sparked from the stars in the heavens.

One of the most prized books of ancient Chinese literature, the I Ching defines fire as a symbol of light and heat that emanates from the sun. It is this radiant light that burns deep inside every person's soul to overcome obstacles with courage, strength and perseverance. The fire that dwells within catapults man's unbridled emotions to fight for what is right and just. Like the Phoenix that rises again and again, the internal flame of the human spirit cannot be extinguished. It is this flame where the innermost emerges and true self is acknowledged. This is a point where we are no longer concerned with earthly attachments and the trappings of society. Fire teaches us to liberate the self and go beyond this world. As the ancient Taoist states; *"Being beyond the world while living in the world"* expresses this point perfectly.

Fire enlightens everything leaving nothing in the shadows. For the Native American Indians fire is a precious gift from Great Spirit. It symbolizes the heart of the people while its smoke carries all prayers to the heavens. The smoke literally becomes the words that touches everything and becomes part of all there is. It is that same fire from the sun that initiates this smoke that brings the essence of spirituality.

Throughout history and still today, the sun represents a symbol of health and happiness. The ancient Egyptians, Aztecs, Romans and Greeks worshipped the sun for its healing powers. They may not have realized the sun was the center of the solar system galaxy, but they did know it was the center of life. Then and now, every living thing on planet earth is in some way sustained by the energy given off by the sun. It is the ultimate star with life giving qualities. With the fire of the sun we blossom as a people. It connects our thoughts to experience and remains attached to the very fabric of our soul.

How Fire Qualities Are Reflected in Human Nature

A universal symbol of light and warmth, fire represents the ability to reach our potential. Like the brilliant, radiant sun, people who possess fire qualities can light up a room with their clarity and brilliance. They need support in order to thrive, which makes fire-types prone to over-attachment, feeling trapped, and manipulation. Non-attachment and patience are essential to preserve their creativity and vision.

Unsupported, however, fire can spiral out of control. And overindulgence can have a negative impact on mental, spiritual, and physical well-being. For this reason, fire people need to practice moderation and seek stable ground, whether personally or professionally. Stability will bring out the best in others and provide a foundation for spiritual awareness.

Fire-types are quick, witty, cheerful, self-reliant, independent, discerning, eager to learn, passionate, attractive, and overly confident. They generally feel everything they do is right and expect others to think the same. This can push people away. They must learn to practice patience and humility in order for their natural charisma and passion to shine through; when they do, fire-types can be a light for themselves and those around them.

Fire is powerful and transformative in nature. Impressive, bold, and expansive, fire people fare best in the public eye. Careers in advertising, public relations, entertainment, fashion, journalism, philosophy, art, justice, and acting are a natural fit.

How to Balance Fire Energy

Fire's brilliance and clarity can have a wonderous impact on society. When taken too far, fire can trigger anxiety and hysterics. Fire people can benefit tremendously from:

- Tai chi or qigong practices, which enhance joint movement and circulation.

- Practicing non-attachment and patience.

- Creating a vision board to reflect dreams.

- A diet rich in leeks, celery, arugula, bamboo shoots, chard, dandelion greens, spinach, tomatoes, brussels sprouts, artichokes, beets, chicory, endive, and lean white meat.

What Can We Learn From Fire?

1. *Clarity.* Fire illuminates and sheds light. When we can see clearly our insight gives us untold power. We become the creator of our own destiny and in the process empower self and others.

2. *Being present.* The fire element represents the "here and now." It teaches us to show up and be present and be consciously aware of the world around us. It reminds us to move away from getting lost in the details and filter through the endless information that can fill our days with nothingness.

3. *To be joyful.* Fire is represented by the summer season and everything about summer spells joy. It is a time of the year where everything comes out to play, flowers are in bloom, and laughter is in the air. Without the element of joy, life is stressful, filled with anxiety and nervous behavior. When we invite joy into our lives we realize each day is a gift waiting to be unwrapped.

4. *Love.* The heart is represented by the element of fire. The warmth and movement of the flame is like a warm heart open to receiving and giving love maintaining a heart to heart connection. When we choose to feel and be felt by others we are in tune with the pure essence of love, kindness, hope and wisdom. This is truly what the heart desires and what happiness is all about.

5. *Power.* A significant level of maturity is how we use power. The element of fire propels us to use power in a constructive manner by having a set of principles and values that guide our use of it. The journey towards conscious and constructive use of power is one of awareness and learning. It is an individual process and one that implores us to move beyond reactive and destructive ways to settle conflicts. The more consciously aware we become the greater our understanding of what true power is.

Meditation for Fire-Types

Fire is characterized by brightness. It represents illumination and consciousness. But its instability can lead to overattachment and addictions. This short meditation is highly effective in loosening the grips of attachment and providing clarity:

- Sit comfortably with your spine erect and shoulders relaxed.

- Focus on the present moment by tuning into the breath.

- Notice where and when your mind wanders, and let go, returning to the present moment.

- Next, breathe in to self-compassion and compassion for others, releasing your attachments. You become bigger than the story in your mind.

- Visualize your suffering and the suffering of others melting away.

Contemplating Fire Energy

The following statements are a result of personal meditations with fire. Take time each day to reflect upon the subtle messages you receive from these meditations.

Monday:

Don't conform in life but rather transform self and others.

Reflection: _____

_____
_____
_____
_____
_____
_____
_____
_____
_____
_____
_____

Contemplating Fire Energy

Reflection: _____

_____
_____
_____
_____
_____
_____
_____
_____
_____
_____
_____
_____
_____
_____
_____
_____
_____
_____
_____
_____
_____
_____

Contemplating Fire Energy

Tuesday:

Be patient to light the flame.

Reflection: _____

_____
_____
_____
_____
_____
_____
_____
_____
_____
_____
_____
_____
_____
_____
_____
_____

Contemplating Fire Energy

Reflection: _____

Contemplating Fire Energy

Wednesday:

Honor and respect my presence. I give plenty but I can take away even more.

Reflection: _____

_____
_____
_____
_____
_____
_____
_____
_____
_____
_____
_____
_____
_____
_____

Contemplating Fire Energy

Reflection: _____

_____
_____
_____
_____
_____
_____
_____
_____
_____
_____
_____
_____
_____
_____
_____
_____
_____
_____
_____
_____
_____
_____
_____

Contemplating Fire Energy

Thursday:

Dance like the flicker of my flame and feel the joy deep within.

Reflection: _____

_____
_____
_____
_____
_____
_____
_____
_____
_____
_____
_____
_____
_____
_____
_____

Contemplating Fire Energy

Reflection: _____

Contemplating Fire Energy

Friday:

I am a beacon of light.

Reflection: _____
_____
_____
_____
_____
_____
_____
_____
_____
_____
_____
_____
_____
_____
_____
_____
_____

Contemplating Fire Energy

Reflection: _____
_____
_____
_____
_____
_____
_____
_____
_____
_____
_____
_____
_____
_____
_____
_____
_____
_____
_____
_____
_____
_____
_____
_____

Contemplating Fire Energy

Saturday:

I am the transformer of all things.

Reflection: _____

_____
_____
_____
_____
_____
_____
_____
_____
_____
_____
_____
_____
_____
_____
_____
_____
_____

Chapter Six :: Fire

Contemplating Fire Energy

Reflection: _____
_____
_____
_____
_____
_____
_____
_____
_____
_____
_____
_____
_____
_____
_____
_____
_____
_____
_____
_____
_____
_____
_____
_____
_____
_____

Contemplating Fire Energy

Sunday:

The more I cling to the more I want.

Reflection: _____

_____
_____
_____
_____
_____
_____
_____
_____
_____
_____
_____
_____
_____
_____
_____

Contemplating Fire Energy

Reflection: _____

_____
_____
_____
_____
_____
_____
_____
_____
_____
_____
_____
_____
_____
_____
_____
_____
_____
_____
_____
_____
_____
_____
_____
_____

Applications

Try the following suggestions to bring the manifestation of fire into your life.

1. Build a fire from scratch.
2. Watch the sun rise and set.
3. Cook a meal over an open fire.
4. Gaze into a flickering candle.
5. Stare at the stars.
6. Feel the warmth of the sun upon your body on a warm summer's day.
7. Listen to the crackling of a log burning.
8. Paint one room in your home a fiery color.
9. Burn your favorite incense.

FIRE

FIRE!

Darkens and thickens,

developing tone

through monstrous roars.

more & more

the land ignites,

glowing embers

and ash.

Flames of protest

We can no longer ignore,

Move

fast.

Calvin Chance

"*Great things are done when men and mountains meet.*"
~*William Blake*

Vancouver, Canada

Seven

Mountain

𝒯he word mountain takes it origin from the Latin word 'Montem' and its use can be dated back to the 13th century. As an intriguing source of nature, mountains have always represented a way to try and reach heaven to access God. This is a major reason why mountains hold a mystical appeal and are part of the stories in many religions. The ancient Chinese actually believed that heaven was literally up in the sky, and that mountains were closer to heaven, making them the best place for meditation and prayer. Taller mountains were actually considered pillars that separated heaven from earth. The belief was that the realm of heaven covered the realm of earth and from this belief arose the idea that heaven could fall down upon the earth. In the ancient myth 'Reparation of Heaven', the Goddess Nu Wa was said to repair the broken sky by killing a giant turtle and erecting its four feet as supporting pillars to the heavens. According to this myth the world was restored to harmony.

Mountains have always been nature's ultimate sign of grandeur. From the times that man was just a cave dweller, till this day, mountains hold the ability to awe us with their sheer beauty and magnificent size. Mountains like Tai Shan in China have been venerated by the Chinese since at least the third millennium BC. Emperors of ancient China regarded Mount Tai Shan as the actual son of the emperor of Heaven. The mountain functioned as God looking down upon his people acting as a communication channel between man and God. Other mountains like Mount Sinai (the mountain of Moses), have miraculous meanings. It is this mountain that Moses came upon a burning bush, unconsumed by its own flames where God spoke to him commanding him to lead his people out of bondage in Egypt and return with them to the mountain. This mountain is the center of a greatly venerated pilgrimage for the Judeo-Christian people.

Shamans, early Taoist and Buddhist monks were also attracted to the mountain. Many were said to live for hundreds of years while taking to the wilderness of the mountains and practicing meditation. Many Buddhist saw the mountain as a silent testimony of the higher source and connection to the divine and dwelling place of a Bodhisattva. These are spiritual beings that have dedicated themselves to the service of assisting all creatures in the transcendence of worldly suffering and attainment of enlightenment. The mountains where the monks and shamans dwelled became known as sacred places and access points to the heavenly realm.

Mountains have always fascinated man pushing the human spirit to conquer their physical heights. It is in the journey and the climb where man seeks to find his soul. Perhaps this is due to the enormous power they hold from their formation or perhaps it is because of the grandeur they silently possess. Either way, man yearns for the silence and stability the mountain offers. By experiencing the mountain with its trees, sounds, rocks and fresh air one can witness its inner strength. It is through inner strength that drives all things in nature; including man himself.

The magnificent size and divine landscape of the mountain is God's gift to man. But as awesome as mountain is, man is God's most prized possession. Man is the final piece of the puzzle, the culmination of all creation. If mountains could speak perhaps they would be in awe of "us" as much as we are in awe of them.

How Mountain Qualities Are Reflected in Human Nature

Mountains possess unwavering strength. Majestic in stature and powerful in nature, they are associated with stability, benevolence, and solidification.

This translates to human qualities of steadiness, persistence, and conservative, methodical thinking. The mountain person is measured, attentive, noble, steadfast, magnanimous, loyal, resolute, and has a strong sense of morality.

However, mountains are formed when tectonic plates collide, sometimes causing destructive volcanic eruptions. This cycle of building and breaking down, which occurs over millions of years, is not unlike the way mountain-types operate: Painstakingly slow and methodical, their often-myopic vison can drive others away.

Mountain energy vacillates between tenderness and greed, and those who identify with its qualities have a tendency to be single-minded, jealous, depressed, and non-resourceful. This will hinder their success if they do not reach out for help from someone more influential and self-assured. Unfortunately, mountain-types are competitive by nature and may deter such help—often the cause for delayed or lack of success. On the other hand, if they are able to seek a mentor, they can easily create superior work and financial status.

The level-headed and persistent nature of mountain energy does receive support from seniors, which makes the mountain person an excellent employee. Jobs that require meticulous attention to detail—archeologists, detectives, researchers, scientists, or strategists—play to the mountain's strengths.

The mountain's stability is associated with contemplative energy and depth. Their ability to focus and tap into their inner selves, or true nature, has the potential to regenerate, change, and revolutionize.

How to Balance Mountain Energy

Mountain's immovable, often stagnant, energy can inhibit creative thought processes. It's important for mountain-types to lighten up and be open to change. Some ways to do that include:

- Daily exercise with an emphasis on stretching and loosening the joints, such as Pilates.

- Walking meditations including labyrinths.

- Taking time for healing massages.

- Learning how to let go of minutiae.

- A diet rich in vegetables and fruits such as asparagus, kohlrabi, sweet potatoes, peppers, broccoli, carrots, apricots, cherries, grapefruit, mangoes, and watermelon.

What Can We Learn From Mountain?

1. *Stillness.* No matter where we are travelling, the mountain remains stationary on the horizon. To the Taoist, the virtue of the mountain is keeping still. When we are still we maintain composure. By maintaining composure we find a greater meaning in each experience and unleash potential power.

2. *Strength.* Life is full of ups and downs. Strength is what helps us get through the rough patches. It defines the limits of everything we do and gives a foundation for life. Only after everything that happens comes one's true nature. When things still affect our being then we have not yet reached a stable inner core like that of the mountain.

3. *Silence.* The mountain represents a transition from between one phase and another, the silent moment between the in breath and the out breath. It is in that space that absolute quietude exists and higher self is revealed. Like the state of meditation, sleep or the first beginning, silence is how we connect to self and others without judgment.

4. *Patience.* The ascent to the top of a mountain requires patience. It teaches us to value the effort and not just the success. It is through patience that we discover who we are and who we are not. Patience leads us to the axis of our being where everything revolves and a cheerful acceptance of life exists. Patience is certainly a virtue that means we can work without expecting a certain outcome.

5. *Peace.* Mountains define the limit of everything we do and when we have done all that we can it is time to rest and find peace. When we are peaceful everything turns around us and yet we do not need to move. From this state we develop patience, inner strength, tolerance, compassion and true happiness.

Meditation for Mountain-Types

*M*ountain's attributes of steadiness, persistence, and precision would benefit from a free-form moving meditation practice. Below is a simple technique to ease their structured focus:

- Begin by standing with your feet hip distance apart. Keep your knees soft with a slight bend and arms loosely to your sides.

- Notice the sensations of your body and your breath. Mind any areas that feel tense. Take several breaths in (count to four) and out slowly (count to four).

- When you're ready, move your arms upwards in front of you as you breathe in and back down as you breathe out; repeat eight times.

- Next, gently twist your body from side to side allowing your arms to swing naturally as you twist. Repeat this motion eight times; inhale and exhale to each side.

- With your arms relaxed at your side, rotate your shoulders slowly several times in both directions. Notice the sensation of your breath.

- Next, gently rotate your head from side to side by dropping your left ear towards your left shoulder. Rotate your head in front of you and drop your right ear towards your right shoulder. Do this slowly and mindfully.

- Finish by shaking your arms and legs out for about 30 seconds. Afterward, stand quietly and focus on the breath. Note the sensations throughout your body.

Contemplating Mountain Energy

The following statements are a result of personal meditations with mountain. Take time each day to reflect upon the subtle messages you receive from these meditations.

Monday:

I am majestic and stand tall for all to see.

Reflection: _____

_____
_____
_____
_____
_____
_____
_____
_____
_____
_____
_____
_____
_____

Chapter Seven :: Mountain

Contemplating Mountain Energy

Reflection: _____

_____
_____
_____
_____
_____
_____
_____
_____
_____
_____
_____
_____
_____
_____
_____
_____
_____
_____
_____
_____
_____
_____
_____

Contemplating Mountain Energy

Tuesday:

My body moves towards the heavens but remains rooted in the earth.

Reflection: _____

_____

_____

_____

_____

_____

_____

_____

_____

_____

_____

_____

_____

_____

_____

Contemplating Mountain Energy

Reflection: _____

_____
_____
_____
_____
_____
_____
_____
_____
_____
_____
_____
_____
_____
_____
_____
_____
_____
_____
_____
_____
_____

Contemplating Mountain Energy

Wednesday:

Listen closely to my hum as it reaches out to the ends of the Universe.

Reflection: _____
_____
_____
_____
_____
_____
_____
_____
_____
_____
_____
_____
_____
_____
_____

Chapter Seven :: Mountain

Contemplating Mountain Energy

Reflection: _____
_____
_____
_____
_____
_____
_____
_____
_____
_____
_____
_____
_____
_____
_____
_____
_____
_____
_____
_____
_____

Contemplating Mountain Energy

Thursday:

I am the culmination of mother earth moving ever so slowly beneath.

Reflection: _____

Contemplating Mountain Energy

Reflection: _____

_____
_____
_____
_____
_____
_____
_____
_____
_____
_____
_____
_____
_____
_____
_____
_____
_____
_____
_____
_____
_____
_____

Contemplating Mountain Energy

Friday:

I am patient and still in spirit and tranquil beyond your wildest dreams.

Reflection: _____
_____
_____
_____
_____
_____
_____
_____
_____
_____
_____
_____
_____
_____
_____
_____

Contemplating Mountain Energy

Reflection: _____

Contemplating Mountain Energy

Saturday:

I am forever reaching higher and welcome those who are up for the challenge.

Reflection: _____

_____

_____

_____

_____

_____

_____

_____

_____

_____

_____

_____

_____

_____

Contemplating Mountain Energy

Reflection: _____

Contemplating Mountain Energy

Sunday:

I am the peace that lies within.

Reflection: _____

_____

_____

_____

_____

_____

_____

_____

_____

_____

_____

_____

_____

_____

_____

_____

Chapter Seven :: Mountain

Contemplating Mountain Energy

Reflection: _____

_____
_____
_____
_____
_____
_____
_____
_____
_____
_____
_____
_____
_____
_____
_____
_____
_____
_____
_____
_____
_____
_____
_____

Applications

The following are some ideas of how you can bring mountain energy into your life.

1. Read about the world's most famous mountains and man's voyages upon them.
2. Visit places with mountain landscapes.
3. Walk a mountain trail.
4. View a mountain range from a plane.
5. Take a gondola ride up a mountain and spend time at the top.
6. Go skiing, sledding or snow-boarding.
7. Sit at the base of a mountain and look up.

MOUNTAIN

Standing

White clouds over

the mountain,

come and go.

And thus we know,

the mountain stands.

Ernest Dempsey

"Every flower is a soul blossoming in nature."
~Gerard De Nerval

Buchart Gardens – Victoria Canada

Eight

Final Thoughts

*N*ot a day goes by that man's eyes will fall upon some part of nature's beauty. The miracle of the sun rising and setting, or the changes in the seasons as they surrender with grace to life's ebb and flow seems so effortless yet profound. Watching the branches of a tree swaying in the breeze, birds whimsically in flight or puffy clouds drifting along the backdrop of a blue sky all make for a colorful palette that awakens our spirit and feeds our soul.

The time is here and now to shift our state of being. Nature is calling us back to Her. She is pleating with us to let go of our ego state of being and to honor the oneness in all things. As man reengages with the natural environment a sense of wholeness will take hold and a new way of living in the world will become apparent. This has always been man's natural state of being it simply has been pushed aside from the materialistic paradigm causing society to think we are separate from nature.

Our very aliveness makes us a part of the ecosystem of the cosmos, just as every other living thing. Nature is what connects us to spiritual source and the gateway to understanding the divine essence in all things and our connection to oneness. Our well-being and overall state of consciousness is dependent on our exposure to nature. The more we interact and surround ourselves with nature's essence the healthier we are in mind, body and spirit.

Communing with nature has a way to energize the spirit, keep us present and experience unexplained joy flowing through the body. One can feel the wind, full of life and intelligence, communicating all around while the sunlight, with all of its warmth and aliveness, energizes everything in its path. There is an intertwining of energy that dances between us and planet earth. We breathe the same air; drink the same water, and share the same underlying essence.

As we bow our heads and give thanks to the grace that surrounds us we expand personal and collective consciousness and as a result there is a death and rebirth of who we are as a species. As the ancient Pawnee Indians so eloquently states in their tribal hymn to Mother Earth:

> Behold! Our Mother Earth is lying here.
>
> Behold! She gives of her fruitfulness
>
> Truly her power she gives us
>
> Give thanks to Mother Earth who lies here.

Nature implores man to embrace life and to cultivate his spirit. As the famous poet and author, Henry David Thoreau stated; "In order for man to take on self-cultivation, he must work with and through nature. It is through nature's wilderness people live sincere lives and awaken the truth."

Chapter Eight :: Final Thoughts

Seeds

The scent of raw ground,

& Crisp

Fresh air.

Swords of grass,

Saluting the seeds; floating

Pollen in the trees.

Free–flowing water,

&

Mud.

It's always been a part of you.

The sun's rays

& the moon

Surround

This rotating planet

called Home.

Calvin Chance

Appendix

▲

Determine Your Force of Nature

Now that you have read through the powerful forces of nature, follow the steps below to determine your personal *Nature Number*.

1. Using the "Theosophical Reduction" process, add the numbers of your birth year together and repeat the process until you have a single digit. For example, 1980 = 1+9+8+0 = 9

2. Subtract this figure from 11. Using the example above, 11 - 9 = 2.

3. There are instances when the number calculated by adding all 4 numbers is 10. For example, the year 1900: 1+9+0+0=10. When reduced to one digit, we are left with a 1, when subtracted from 11 is 10. The solution is to reduce the number to a single digit: 11 – 1 = 10, 1+ 0 = 1.

4. Refer to the "Force of Nature Number Table" on page 169 to find out what aspect of nature resonates with you.

Special Note If you were born between 1 January and 3 February, use the preceding year to find your nature number. For example, born January 9th, 1989 use 1988 as the year for your calculation.

Appendix

Force of Nature Number Table:

Force of Nature Number 1 or 7: Refer to Water Energy

Force of Nature Number 2: Refer to Mother Earth Energy

Force of Nature Number 3: Refer to Tree Energy

Force of Nature Number 4: Refer to Wind Energy

Force of Nature Number 5: Female refer to Mother Earth Energy and Male refer to Mountain Energy

Force of Nature Number 6: Refer to Sky Energy

Force of Nature Number 8: Refer to Mountain Energy

Force of Nature Number 9: Refer to Fire Energy

About the Author

Mary Jane (MJ) Kasliner, is an author, teacher, lifestyle master and creator of Codes of Creation in Movement®.

Since 1985, MJ has dedicated her career to helping others improve their health and well-being. She started her professional life as a Respiratory Therapist and Dental Hygienist before she made the radical shift into the world of Metaphysics.

Her big career move occurred in 2002, and she has been astounded ever since by the transformation of her readers and clients alike who incorporate her lifestyle strategies into their lives.

Education

Mary Jane graduated from Skidmore College with a degree in Health Science and Union College with a degree in Applied Sciences. She studied Western Feng Shui at the De Amicis School in Philadelphia and Classical Feng Shui at the New York School of Feng Shui and Feng Shui Institute of London. Over the years, Mary Jane has helped many clients, including some of Manhattan's elite to transform their lives through the power of attraction in design.

Mary Jane's yoga trainings are comprehensive including Vinyasa, Anusara, Bridge to Lotus, Mastery of Meditation, Chakra Therapy and her signature Registered Trademark *Codes of Creation in Movement®*.

Mary Jane believes in giving back to the world for human welfare. MJ was honored to be a part of Sean Corn's *Off the Mat and Into the World*

About the Author

humanitarian effort to Uganda where she raised thousands of dollars for orphaned children due to war and AIDS.

Mary Jane has received worldwide media coverage from the Associated Press for her work. She has been interviewed on TV and radio and is the author of 9 books, a DIY design platform that weaves the power of attraction into one's life, and a lifestyle coach guiding students through her *Codes of Creation Mastermind System.*

Mary Jane loves to play golf and travel in her spare time. She can be contacted at www.mjkasliner.com.

About the Poets

Calvin Chance is currently recording his debut album free.WORLD., featuring songs recorded internationally, from Dubai to Eugene. An entrepreneur, he manages the OverseeRs International Artistic Collective (based out of Dubai, UAE). Back in Oregon, he has been busy co-founding Live the Dream Productions. His debut poetry book, also titled free.WORLD., will be released shortly before his album in the summer of 2013. An aspiring writer, designer and musician - art is Calvin's life and obsession. You can stay in touch with calvin/CHANCE's career through his online social media sites.

Ernest Dempsey edits the quarterly journal *Recovering the Self* (http://www.recoveringself.com/) published from Michigan and also contributes to the *Journal of Humanitarian Affairs* (http://greenheritagenews.com/). He has published four books including his story book *The Blue Fairy and Other Tales of Transcendence* (Modern History Press, 2010). His poetry book *Two Candles* is coming out this summer in Texas. He has also worked as a citizen journalist and a freelance proofreader and editor. Dempsey is vegetarian and an animal rights activist. Currently he is based in Oregon and enjoys his time writing and blogging.

Christina Garofalo was raised at the Jersey Shore and graduated from Muhlenberg College with a Bachelor of Arts in English and a minor in studio art. Her poems capture daily life through an ironic feminist voice and have appeared in Muhlenberg College's annual literary publication, *Muses*. Christina is currently a staff writer and editor at *Robb Report* and a regular contributor to FirstWeFeast.com. In her spare time, she is eating her way through Brooklyn, New York, where she lives with her two roommates and a signed photo of Scully and Mulder. Her other interests include travel, foreign languages, contemporary artwork, and music.

Renae Johnson is an educator at heart, enjoying a 40 year career as a corporate trainer and instructional designer. In addition, she and her husband have written and published 12 books of curriculum on developing personal values, such as honesty, gratitude, and joyfulness. In 2011, Renae experienced a stroke, which paralyzed the right half of her body. Despite this setback, or perhaps because of it, Renae has sought a way to channel her creative voice and her educator mindset. Her writing, while personally reflective, always seeks to bring herself and the reader into a learning experience of self-discovery. Renae can be reached via email: renaebuttonjohnson@gmail.com.

Ralph Roggenbuck earned an associate's degree in elementary education from Minot State University and later a B.A. in University Studies from there. His work history is long and varied; including professional, service industries, factory work, sales, agricultural, and entrepreneurial factors. He has been writing on a semi-professional level for about 15 years. This includes several national magazine articles and some on-line publications. Contacting is easy, through his personal website www.aeontoys.weebly.com or by email at ralbuck@yahoo.com.

About the Cover Illustrator

▲

Illustrator and visual artist, **Tara Barnett** draws inspiration from natural elements, lyrical imagery and personal experience. She has studied at Otis, F.I.T., and SCAD before attaining her BFA in Illustration from Parsons the New School for Design. Recently, Tara organized the publication of Barbara Nessim's An Artful Life and assisted in creating her exhibition, under the same name, at the Victoria and Albert Museum in London. Tara continues working out of New York, rewriting traditions and portraying her distinct voice through pencil, oil, and acrylic. She is also studying Art Education where she hopes to bring her knowledge and experience to help nurture and teach the minds of young artists developing their passion.

Bibliography

Emoto, Masaru. The Hidden Messages in Water. Atria Books, 2005.

Green, Roger. The I Ching Workbook. New Holland, 2004.

Hartdegen, Stephen. The New American Bible. World Catholic Press – A Division of World Bible Publishers. , 1987.

Olds, Glenn, Dr. Chief Seattle's Thoughts. Reprint from Alaska's Future Frontiers Conference, 1979. World Wide Web, 2012.

Tzu, Lao. Tao te Ching. (Translated by Brian Browne Walker). St. Martins Press, 1996.

Sandifer, Jon & Yang, Wang, Dr. The Authentic I Ching. Watkins Publishing London, 2003.

Wikipedia. The free encyclopedia. World Wide Web. The White Tree of Gondor. June 2012 last edited page.

Wordsworth, William. "Tintern Abbey." An Anthology. 3rd Ed. ED. Duncan Wu. Oxford: Blackwell 2006.

World Wide Web. The Great Religions of the World. Barefoot's World.

Credits and Permissions

All photos copyright © Mary Jane Kasliner.

All meditations copyright © Mary Jane Kasliner.

All quotes in opening chapters are granted permission by the "Fair Use" act.

Poems granted permission by Poets:

Calvin Chance

Ernest Dempsey

Christina Garofalo

Renae Johnson

Ralph Roggenbuck

www.ingramcontent.com/pod-product-compliance
Lightning Source LLC
Chambersburg PA
CBHW070602020526
44112CB00050B/2355